Contents

Some words are shown in bold, **like this.** You can find out what they mean by looking in the glossary.

Road roller

Heavy road rollers are used to repair roads and paths. They flatten hot tar to make the ground **level**.

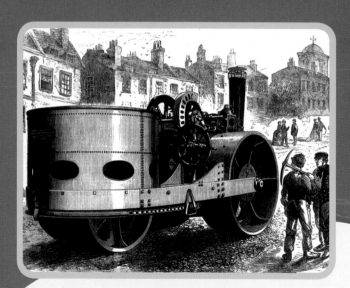

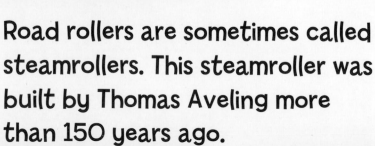

Road rollers are sometimes called steamrollers. This steamroller was built by Thomas Aveling more than 150 years ago.

roller

tar

Punch power

This machine is a huge hammer called a hydraulic hammer. It breaks up rocks and **concrete**.

Hydraulic hammers are also called breakers or hoe rams.

Heavy truck

Meet one of the world's largest dumper trucks. It is used to carry soil on mining sites.

This truck can haul 368 metric tons (406 tons). That's the same as carrying 66 adult elephants!

Big bulldozer

A bulldozer's huge **blade** shoves away massive amounts of **rubble**, rock, and soil.

The biggest bulldozer in the world is as large as a house!

blade

Flying high

The world's tallest crane is 248 metres (814 feet) tall. It's the height of about 50 giraffes standing on top of each other!

Super
Big
Mighty
Size

This crane can lift about 600 metric tons (661 tons). That's as many as 350 cars at once!

Super scoop

The world's largest shovel can carry 85 metric tons (94 tons). That's the same as lifting about 50 cars at once!

groove

The **grooves** on these thick tyres help to grip bumpy ground.

15

crazy crusher

This huge machine is called a crusher. It is used to break up large rocks into **gravel**.

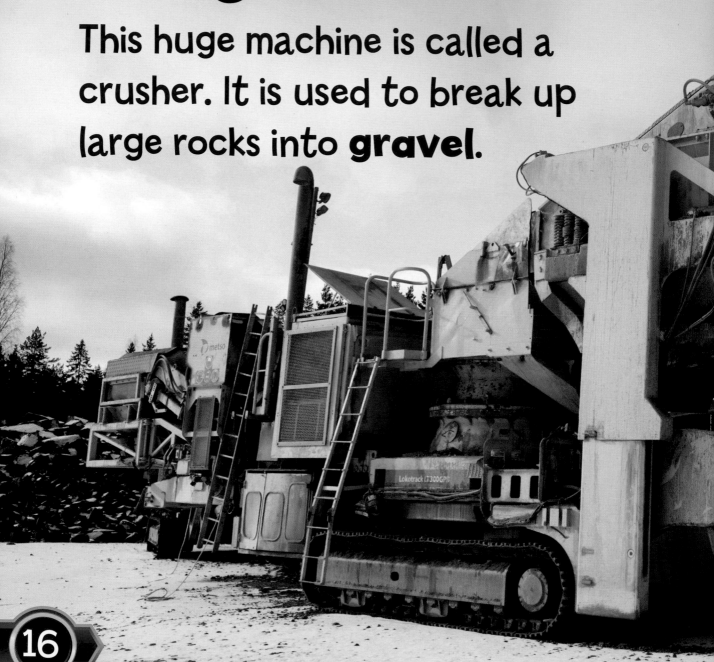

Lokotrack LT300GP

metso

Deep digger

Check out this giant digging machine, or **excavator**. Its 20 buckets scoop up coal. The buckets are so big that one accidentally picked up a bulldozer once!

The digger is so heavy that when it is driven over roads, the roads are destroyed.

Super

Big

Mighty

Size

buckets

19

Sizing things up

Road Roller

Weight	up to 12 metric tons (13 tons)
Height.	up to 3 metres (10 feet)
Drum length	up to 2 metres (6.6 feet)
Tyre width	up to 2.7 metres (8.9 feet)
Engine.	137 horsepower

drum

Weight	up to 26 metric tons (29 tons)
Height	up to 4.4 metres (14.5 feet)
Blade weight	up to 7.3 metric tons (8 tons)
Track length	4 metres (13 feet)
Engine	up to 266 horsepower

Bulldozer

blade

Quiz

How much of a Machine Mega-Brain are you?
Can you match each machine name to its correct photo?

**excavator • crusher
bulldozer • crane**

1

2

3

4

22

Check the answers on the opposite page
to see if you got all four correct.

Glossary

blade the cutting part of a machine that has a thin, sharp edge

concrete a mixture of cement, water, sand, and gravel that hardens when dry

excavator a machine that is used for digging

gravel a mixture of sand, pebbles, and broken rocks

groove a long, narrow channel cut into a surface

level to make something flat

rubble the broken pieces that are left when a building falls down

Find out more

Books

Demolition, Sally Sutton (Candlewick Press, 2012)

Diggers (Mighty Machines), Amanda Askew (QED Publishing, 2011)

Websites

www.jcbexplore.com
www.uk.cat.com/equipment

Index